THE TIES THAT BIND

A Pair of One-Act Plays
by
REGINA TAYLOR

WATERMELON RINDS
and
INSIDE THE BELLY OF THE BEAST

Dramatic Publishing
Woodstock, Illinois • London, England • Melbourne, Australia

*** NOTICE ***

The amateur and stock acting rights to this work are controlled exclusively by THE DRAMATIC PUBLISHING COMPANY without whose permission in writing no performance of it may be given. Royalty fees are given in our current catalogue and are subject to change without notice. Royalty must be paid every time a play is performed whether or not it is presented for profit and whether or not admission is charged. A play is performed anytime it is acted before an audience. All inquiries concerning amateur and stock rights should be addressed to:

DRAMATIC PUBLISHING
P. O. Box 129, Woodstock, Illinois 60098.

COPYRIGHT LAW GIVES THE AUTHOR OR THE AUTHOR'S AGENT THE EXCLUSIVE RIGHT TO MAKE COPIES. This law provides authors with a fair return for their creative efforts. Authors earn their living from the royalties they receive from book sales and from the performance of their work. Conscientious observance of copyright law is not only ethical, it encourages authors to continue their creative work. This work is fully protected by copyright. No alterations, deletions or substitutions may be made in the work without the prior written consent of the publisher. No part of this work may be reproduced or transmitted in any form or by any means, electronic or mechanical, including photocopy, recording, videotape, film, or any information storage and retrieval system, without permission in writing from the publisher. It may not be performed either by professionals or amateurs without payment of royalty. All rights, including but not limited to the professional, motion picture, radio, television, videotape, foreign language, tabloid, recitation, lecturing, publication, and reading are reserved. *On all programs this notice should appear:*

"Produced by special arrangement with
THE DRAMATIC PUBLISHING COMPANY of Woodstock, Illinois"

©MCMXCIII, MCMXCV by
REGINA TAYLOR

Printed in the United States of America
All Rights Reserved
(THE TIES THAT BIND)

Cover design by Susan Carle

ISBN 0-87129-519-9

Contents

WATERMELON RINDS   5
INSIDE THE BELLY OF THE BEAST   47

THE TIES THAT BIND was originally produced by
The Goodman Theatre, Chicago, Illinois
on April 18, 1994

WATERMELON RINDS

for Novella Nelson and the Louisville cast—
and special thanks, Mom

The Actors Theatre of Louisville's 17th Annual Humana Festival of New American Plays (February 25-April 4, 1993) presented *WATERMELON RINDS* with the following artists:

CAST

Jes Semple	Roger Robinson
Lottie Semple	Kalimi A. Baxter
Willy Semple	Donald Griffin
Liza Semple	Regina Byrd Smith
Pinkie Semple	Elain Graham
Papa Tommy Semple	Ray Johnson
Mama Pearl Semple	Yvette Hawkins
Marva Semple-Weisse	Judy Tate

Directed by	Novella Nelson
Scenic Designer	Paul Owen
Costume Designer	Toni-Leslie James
Lighting Designer	Marcus Dilliard
Sound Designer	Casey L. Warren
Props Master	Mark J. Bissonnette
Stage Manager	Frazier W. Marsh
Ass't. Stage Manager	Lori M. Doyle
2nd Ass't. Stage Manager	Emily Fox
Movement Supervisor	Ervon Neely
Production Dramaturg	Michael Bigelow Dixon
Casting arranged by	Judy Dennis

WATERMELON RINDS

A Play in One Act
For Three Men and Five Women

CHARACTERS

JES SEMPLE
LOTTIE SEMPLE
WILLY SEMPLE
LIZA SEMPLE
PINKIE SEMPLE
MAMA PEARL SEMPLE
PAPA TOMMY SEMPLE
MARVA SEMPLE-WEISSE

THE TIME: The present.

THE PLACE: A household in an urban neighborhood.

WATERMELON RINDS

SCENE ONE

(JES stands in spotlight DR.)

I don't like to go to plays. I'd rather sit on the corner and play poker, a little dominoes, talk loud at passing women, watch cats copulating on the sidewalk, turn up the volume and do the loose goose...or do the nasty with a lady whose butt costs less than the price of a g-d theater ticket.

I bought a theater ticket once. The paper said it was a black comedy. I went inside. I sat there for two hours. I didn't see one black. And it sure wasn't a comedy. Just a bunch of white people talking about throwing babies out with their bath water and putting hedgehogs up their you-know-whats. (Excuse me, ladies.) But as I said, this ain't no black comedy. This is absurd. Then I got up and walked out. *(Blackout.)*

SCENE TWO

(Lights come up on a living room stacked high with articles of living...clothes, books, furniture, a candelabra, old toy baby carriage...everything including the kitchen sink. Boxes are scattered. Some empty, half-full, and full, taped, and labeled—POTTERY, LOTTIE'S CLOTHES, BAR-B-QUE GRILL, SAM, etc. There is a clearing that leads off R to the kitchen. Another path leads to a door UL to the other parts of the house. Off L is the door to the outside. DL is a window.

LOTTIE, fourteen years old, wearing a white slip that shows her newly-budding form, is standing on the table doing a barefoot softshoe.)

LOTTIE *(singing cheerfully)*. YANG YANG YANG YANG. YANG YANG YANG. *(A knocking on the door.)* I'll get it.

WILLY *(offstage)*. Don't touch that door. Nobody lives here. We're moving.

LIZA *(offstage)*. Are they here already? Everything isn't prepared yet.

WILLY *(offstage)*. You never know who's on the other side—

LIZA *(offstage)*. Lottie, are you dressed yet?

WILLY *(offstage)*. Damn BEAN EATERS.

LIZA *(offstage.)* If they're here and you're not dressed yet... *(More knocking.)*

LOTTIE. Who's there?

JES *(offstage)*. Jes.

LOTTIE. Jes who?

JES *(offstage)*. Jes me and my shadow...Let me in.

(LOTTIE opens the door. JES is there.)

JES *(his best Groucho Marx imitation).* This country club once refused me entrance. I said—Fine, I don't want to join any club that would have me for a member. They said —their swimming pool was for whites only—I said my great-great-grandmother was raped by her slave master—I'm part white—can I go in up to my knees?
LIZA *(offstage).* Is anyone here yet?
LOTTIE. No, ma'am.
JES. I'm hungry. When we were growing up we were so po'—our parents had to sleep in the same bed. We were so po'...

(WILLY enters from UR carrying a bundle and a box. He begins sorting.)

WILLY. They'll all come, they'll eat, they'll leave, we'll move. Get off the table, Lottie.
LOTTIE. Guess who I am. *(Tapping and singing.)* YANG YANG YANG YANG. YANG YANG YANG.
WILLY. You're my daughter, is who.
JES. Though a man can never tell for sure—
LOTTIE. No. Not your daughter.
JES. A woman can tell a man anything.
LOTTIE. Shirley Temple. Get it?
JES. Shirley Temple Black.
LOTTIE. Shirley Temple in *The Blue Bird of Happiness.*
WILLY. Shirley-going-to-get-her-butt-beat-for-dancing-on-the-table-when-I-told-her-to-get-off-Temple. *(LOTTIE gets off the table.)*
JES. You may be Shirley but your hips are Monroe. Girl, you are getting as big as your mama.

LIZA *(offstage).* I know I'm not known for my cooking but this is a special occasion. I can feel it. *(Then:)* Lottie, are you dressed yet? You're getting too big to run around with nothing on. *(LOTTIE takes two nickels and drops them down the front of her slip and sticks out her chest.)*

LOTTIE. TA-DA! They didn't fall down. Get it?

JES. Do you know another one?

LIZA *(offstage).* They'll be here any minute and if you're not dressed yet...*(JES takes a glass, puts it to LOTTIE's elbow, pumps her arm and the glass fills with milk.*)*

LOTTIE. How did you do that?

LIZA *(offstage).* Heard of a girl abducted, half-naked from her own house...*(JES drinks the milk.)*

LOTTIE. How?

LIZA *(offstage).* ...never seen again.

JES. I'll tell you the secret when you get older.

LIZA *(offstage).* Found out later that it was a member of her own family.

LOTTIE. I don't want to ever grow up. Do you remember Shirley Temple in *The Blue Bird of Happiness*?

JES. *Blue Bird of Happiness*? Isn't that the one with Bill "Bojangles" Robinson? She used to do a lot of films with old Bojangles. He was one of the best tap dancers in the world. They attributed it to his big feet. What else can you do with feet that big? I heard he taught little Miss Shirley everything she knew about dancing. And how she loved to dance with her Bojangles. Sweet, black, big-footed Bojangles. Always smiling, both of them together—dancing and smiling—That's why they took him away.

LOTTIE. Who did?

JES. When they found out why they were always grinning— they dragged him away, kicking, and cut off his—

---

* *Check magic shop—one suggestion might be to use a two-sided glass.*

WILLY. JES!

JES. His feet. Nigger with all that rhythm and no feet—what's he going to do?

LOTTIE. That's not funny, Uncle Jes.

JES. Bojangles didn't think it was funny either. Can't tap with your hands—though some have tried—just can't get the same kind of satisfaction. *(We hear a round of firecrackers. LOTTIE runs to the window.)*

WILLY. Damn Bean Eaters!

JES. Blow your hands off—Don't come crying to me.

WILLY. That's why we're moving.

JES. "Don't come crying to me." That's what they used to say.

WILLY. Lottie, get away from that window.

LOTTIE. It was so pretty. It shot straight up—a bright red ball—and exploded in mid-air. It sprinkled down like rain. Red rain...

JES. "Blow your hands off..."

WILLY. I don't want you going out of this house today, Lottie.

LOTTIE. You never want me to go out.

WILLY. Damn neighborhood. BEAN EATERS—try to find any excuse for disturbing my peace of mind. *(To LOTTIE.)* I don't want you to talk to them, touch them, look at them directly. *(Then:)* That's why we're moving.

LOTTIE. When are we moving?

WILLY. Soon. Very soon. Leave everything behind. It's just going to be good things for my little blue bird. *(Tying up the box he has been filling.)* Boxes. Everything I own, memories, conversations—in these boxes. Shit. Tombs. I've been sitting in the same spot, the exact same spot for the last twenty years and steadily progressing backwards. How can that be? This used to be my favorite shirt. What's left of it...rags...pieces of something else...

JES. Heard you got King Tut's tiara stashed away up in there.
WILLY. Maybe...but damned if I can remember which box.
JES. Ain't that the way it goes?
WILLY. One day real soon we're going to move—move forward—move out and get us a big mansion for my little blue bird. Sacrifices have been made and it's any moment now.
JES. People can't move forward without some sacrifice.
WILLY. Mortgages, loans, scraping, saving, hard work.
JES. Man knew from the beginning. While beating on their drums, and getting high on mooloo juice—they dipped their bodies in monkey fat and danced—danced until the earth gave way to valleys. While praying to their gods they burned sacred offerings...
LIZA *(offstage)*. Fried chicken...bar-b-que ribs...smoked ham...
JES. ...the fatted calf, the lamb, the first-born male, the virgin.
LOTTIE. Everybody is coming today. YANG YANG YANG YANG.
LIZA *(offstage)*. ...pickled pig's feet...ox-tail stew...hog head cheese...I know I'm not known for my cooking but I've really outdone myself today.
WILLY. She used to be able to cook.
LIZA *(offstage)*. Mmmm. It smells good in here.
WILLY. That's why I married her.
LIZA *(offstage)*. Get out of here. I don't want anyone peeping into my kitchen until I'm ready. You're going to be so proud.
WILLY. Every Friday and Saturday, this was before I proposed, she would lure me into her kitchen with a promise of a taste from her pot.
LIZA *(offstage)*. Remember those things I used to fix for you, Willy? I'm feeling it again.

WILLY. Yes, Liza.

LIZA *(offstage)*. You don't believe me, do you? Man doesn't believe anything until it's rolling around on his tongue. You'll see.

WILLY *(hopeful)*. It is beginning to smell...

LOTTIE. I smell something.

JES. I'm hungry enough. *(WILLY picks up another bundle and exits.)* When we were growing up, we were so po'—our termites reported us to the Better Housing Bureau. We were so po'—we'd wait until the lights went out and stole the leftovers from our rat's pantry. We were so po'—No, po' ain't funny, there is nothing funny about being po'—We were so po' that fourteen of us had to sleep in one bed while the rest slept on the floor—which was pretty difficult considering that we were so po' we couldn't afford a house with indoor plumbing—so po' we lived in the outhouse. We lived in an outhouse so small that those sleeping on the floor were likely to fall into the hole if they weren't careful. Those sleeping on the floor learned to hold on to each other and the walls. But every once in awhile you would be awakened in the middle of the night by a surprised echoing scream and you'd know another brother or sister had let go or was pushed and was lost in that bottomless stinky pit. They said that if you were lucky that you would fall straight to China. If you were lucky. We were so po'—we had a dog once. We named him Lucky. He starved to death. Lucky—we ate him. I did keep a pet cockroach. He was as big as a dog. Named him Rex. Walked him on a leash. Ever try to teach a cockroach to roll over and play dead? Ever try to curb a roach? Which leg does he raise? Listen, Lottie—we were so po'—we had to devour our own in order to survive. Do you know what c-a-n-n-i-b-u-l-l spells?

(We hear firecrackers. JES falls to the floor and convulses as if he were repeatedly shot. WILLY re-enters, carrying another box.)

WILLY. Damn bean eaters.

LOTTIE *(watching JES convulse)*. Are you dead yet? Uncle Jes is such a riot.

JES *(finally)*. Hear that?—'NAM.

LOTTIE. Were you in 'Nam, Uncle Jes?

WILLY. That's why we're moving.

JES. The summer of '68. Hot, white beach. Beirut.

WILLY. You were never in Beirut. Shooting, killing, raping.

LOTTIE. That's what it's like in Beirut?

WILLY. This neighborhood. Bean eaters with their ghetto blasters and uzis.

JES. If I wasn't in El Salvador—then—what happened to my hands? *(JES loses his hands up his sleeves and chases LOTTIE—screaming—around the room.)*

WILLY. The real estate man said that we were buying into a good solid middle-class neighborhood. We moved in. The first on the block. Fine. A couple of families moved out. Fine. Next thing you know—another black family wants to move in. White flight. They flew. Mass exodus. The next thing you know—any kind of nigger and his pit bull is moving in. Drug dealers, bean eaters and their pet cockroaches big enough to walk on leashes. If I wanted to buy into a ghetto—I would never have moved. This is not what was promised. Sacrifices have been made.

JES. When we were growing up, we were so po'—

WILLY. We were never *poor*. Yes, we had to struggle, but we were never poor. Anything worth anything is worth some sacrifice. Remember that, Lottie.

JES. We weren't poor. We were so po' we couldn't afford the extra o and r. Ever been to a all-white beach in Alabama with a sign on it—"No dogs or coloreds allowed"?

WILLY. ...can he go in up to his knees...

LOTTIE. That's how it was in the old days?

WILLY. They don't have beaches in Alabama.

JES. 1968. Hot, white beach. Alabama. He said, "Boy, what you doing on this here beach?" I said, "Boy? Who are you talking to?" And he and his friends took out these knives, long enough for shish-ke-bobin', and he says, "I'm talking to you, nigger." And that is how I lost my hands down a white woman's bikini in Alabamy. *(JES loses his hands up his sleeves and chases LOTTIE—screaming—around the room.)*

WILLY. First on the block.

JES. No, I've never been to Iraq.

WILLY. Should have been the last.

JES. But I know how it feels.

LIZA *(offstage, singing)*.
> There is a fountain filled with blood,
> Drawn from Emanuel's veins...
> And sinners plunged beneath that flood, lose all their guilt and stain.
> Lose all their guilt and stain, lose all their guilt and stain.
> And sinners plunged beneath that flood, lose all their guilt and stain.

WILLY *(hopeful)*. It's been a long time since I heard her singing in the kitchen. *(We hear a knocking on the door.)*

LOTTIE. Who's there?

PINKIE *(offstage)*. The big bad wolf. Let me in.

LOTTIE. Not by the hair on my chinny, chin, chin.

PINKIE *(offstage)*. Your chin, my ass. Girl, open this door.

(LOTTIE opens the door and PINKIE enters. She is very pregnant.)

WILLY. Well look what the cat dragged in.

PINKIE. Boy, don't get started with me. I came here to celebrate, to have a good time. This time I'm going to have a nice time with my family. *(To LOTTIE.)* Look at this girl, getting so healthy and fat. I see the bees done bit.

JES. You can't talk about getting fat...

PINKIE *(rubbing her belly)*. ...any minute now.

WILLY. What's the count up to now? Every time I see you, you're pregnant. What do you do, Pinkie?

PINKIE. Well if you don't know—I'm not going to tell you.

JES. Where are the rest of them?

PINKIE. Left them at home. You know my kids...

WILLY. Wild and untamed.

PINKIE. I see you redecorated the place.

WILLY. We're moving any day.

PINKIE. I heard that before. When are we going to eat?

LOTTIE. You know how slow Mama is.

PINKIE. Ain't you fast? Why aren't you in there helping?

LOTTIE. She said that she didn't want any help. *(We hear a crash of pots and dishes.)*

PINKIE. Liza, are you all right in there?

LIZA *(offstage)*. Pinkie! I'm just fine. Everything is fine in here. Never mind me. Any minute, and we'll be feasting at a banquet.

PINKIE. All right, then...*(Lower.)* I hope you got a McDonald's nearby. I'm hungry. My feet hurt and my back. *(She rubs her stomach.)* I might name this one—Jessee.

WILLY. I don't want to hear it

PINKIE. I didn't say nothing. Let me hush. But this one is going to turn out.

WILLY. Just like your other ones.
PINKIE. They just weren't inspired. They had it in them but they just weren't inspired.
WILLY. Where is little Lumumba?
PINKIE. Big Lumumba. He hasn't written to me in a long time.
WILLY. And coke-head Marion? Heard Eldridge went crazy—
PINKIE. He was a hyperactive child...
WILLY. Carmichael fled the country...George was in a shoot-out in prison.
PINKIE. He's dead. They were just born in the wrong time, is all. That's what I figure. The time wasn't right. Not for them. But this one—by the time he gets through puberty... *(She notices LOTTIE staring at her belly.)* You never seen a pregnant woman before? Do you want to rub my belly? *(LOTTIE places her hands on PINKIE's stomach. Then, startled, LOTTIE jerks away.)* Don't be scared. That's just him saying hello. *(To her belly.)* What's that? You saying, "Who's that rubbing on Mama's belly?" That's your cousin, Lottie...No, you haven't met her before.
LOTTIE. He can hear you?
PINKIE. Of course he can. Talk to you too—if you want to get to know him better. He'll talk your ear off.
LOTTIE *(her head on PINKIE's belly)*. I can hear him breathing.
WILLY. Unborn babies don't breathe, Lottie.
PINKIE. Who are you—Dr. Spock? The girl knows what she hears.
LOTTIE. I think I can make out...he's saying something...but it's too low.
PINKIE. He can be a bit soft-spoken.
WILLY. I may not be a pediatrician but most fetuses don't speak.

PINKIE. That's brilliant, Sherlock. Most don't. I think I'll name him X.
JES. X. I like that.
WILLY. First, Jessee and now—X. As far as I know Malcolm X died a long time ago. Just who are you claiming this child is by?
PINKIE. Do you really want to know? I didn't think so.
JES. X Semple. I like that.
PINKIE. Thank you.
WILLY. And how do you know it's going to be a boy?
PINKIE. How does every mother know?
WILLY. Oh, he told you.
PINKIE. He didn't have to...He isn't just kicking up in there...I can feel him. Three-inch erections pounding against my womb, four or five times a day. That's how I know.
WILLY. Three inches!...Four or five...Pinkie!
PINKIE. I suppose you're going to tell me that it's not possible. How would you know? You've never been pregnant.
WILLY. My wife has and she never told me...
PINKIE. How would she know? The only child she had was a girl. X Semple. Finally, a manchild to do credit to this family.
WILLY. And what does that mean?
PINKIE. I mean, that not since our brother Sam, as stupid as he was, has there been a Semple man in this family worth the salt he pees.
WILLY. Wait a minute...
PINKIE. Let me hush. I came here to celebrate and have a good time with my family.
LOTTIE. I can feel it. It is a boy...Daddy...it IS a boy!
WILLY. Lottie, take your hands off this second.
PINKIE. Yeah, that's him. Just humping away.
LOTTIE. I felt him!

WILLY. Didn't your mother tell you to go get dressed? Go get dressed, Lottie.

PINKIE *(rocking)*. Um-um...that's my boy...mmm-hmm. *(LOTTIE reluctantly exits.)* Why do you want to send Lottie out, Willy. She's a woman now. There are things she needs to know. You always have been protective.

WILLY. She's still a child.

(LOTTIE is in her room, dressing.)

LOTTIE. When the hens come home...Sometimes the voices come from outside. My parents. At night I can hear them through the walls. Sometimes I hear the walls quaking, banging. Their voices rise and fall in arias. On the other side. Of the wall. The sheets flapping. Flapping above them. And the beating of bird wings against its bars. In those mornings I sneak into their room. After they've risen. And search the room. The closets, between the bedcovers...searching for signs...feathers of the slaughtered birds. Sometimes I find a spot of blood and always the fresh smell of death. Yang, yang, yang, yang, yang, yang, yang. When the roosters come home? When the chickens...What Pinkie's baby whispered in my ear...Sometimes the voices come from outside. On the other side. Out there. Like low-flying helicopters, their voices. One day—looking out. Three boys talking loud and throwing bottles against the wall. One was black as midnight. One with coiled snakes hissing all over his head. And the third tall and sinewy like a swaying palm. The first one saw me spying and smiled at me. His teeth glistened with gold. Rapunzel, Rapunzel, let down your golden hair. And he climbed up to her ivory tower...Sometimes the voices come from inside me. Clear as a bell. She was a poor peasant girl and barely thirteen when she saw the visions and heard the voices that told her to pick up the shield and sword and march to...New Orleans? One day my voices will tell me what and when. My voices will explode. The walls will be knocked down. And you'll see freedom flapping its wings and crowing. When the morning comes.

WILLY. Some things she doesn't need to know. Not now.

PINKIE. Then when?

WILLY. Some things she doesn't ever have to know about. Not like we knew them. No need. Some things she never needs to hear, see or touch.

PINKIE. No pain, no gain.

WILLY. The things we went through—I went through so she would never have to. I cherish her, protect her, fight for my destiny.

PINKIE. One day she'll have to learn to fight for herself. Locking her in her room isn't going to help. It's just going to make the lessons she's going to have to learn just that much harder.

WILLY. Yeah, you know all about it.

PINKIE. That's right. I have the proof of my life experience written all over my body. From stretch marks to razor scars from a drunken lover...I still have the welts on my back which were the gifts from our dear parents.

WILLY. Our parents never beat us.

PINKIE. That's how bad they beat you—BRAIN DAMAGE. You can't even remember. I remember—Mama tried to break my neck, one time.

WILLY. If only she had broken your tongue.

PINKIE. You know it's true.

WILLY. The only time our parents laid hand on us was in love.

PINKIE. They loved to lay hand on me, fist on me, extension cord...frying pan.

WILLY. It wasn't so bad. Though, there was this time when Daddy chased Jes with a baseball bat.

JES *(to audience)*. Yeah, yeah...I gave him a good run. He was fast back then. I ran into the park and lost him around the lake.

WILLY. You had to came back home sometime.

PINKIE. Daddy sat patiently on the porch.

JES *(to audience)*. For three days.

PINKIE. Three hours. Dinnertime, you came home.

WILLY. Slunk home with your tail tucked between your legs.

JES *(to audience)*. He said, "Boy, are you ready?" "Yes, sir." "Then, get in the house and let down the shades and then let down your pants."

PINKIE *(sarcastic)*. They only laid hands on us in love.

JES *(to audience)*. "This is going to hurt me more than you. I'm only starting what the MAN is going to finish."

WILLY *(to audience)*. He always said that we couldn't afford to be lazy and undisciplined. That's what *they* expected from us. And he came down harder on us for living up to their expectations. That was the world. That's what I learned from the whuppings.

PINKIE *(to audience)*. Your own will treat you as bad or worse than anyone else. That's what I learned.

WILLY. Pinkie...

PINKIE. Sam never got any licks.

JES. I sure do miss Sam.

WILLY. He was always the favorite.

PINKIE. He should have been. He was a saint, as stupid as he was.

WILLY. Like the time he fell out of the treehouse.

JES *(to audience)*. ...Some got lost down the hole...

PINKIE *(to audience)*. Jes pushed him.
JES *(to audience)*. He jumped.
PINKIE. I was in the house cleaning up after you lazy lunkheads, as usual, when I heard his scream. I never will forget it.
WILLY. I had gone to the candy shop and left Jes up in the treehouse with little Sammy. I heard him five blocks away...
PINKIE. I ran to the backyard, yelling, "What's going on?" and there was little Sam lying flat on the ground.
JES. He just jumped.
PINKIE. And Jes was up in the treehouse, looking down, laughing.
JES. I told him not to.
PINKIE. Just laughing your head off.
JES *(to audience)*. We were playing—Tarzan—and he was Cheetah. I lost my balance and the next thing I knew—he had flung himself off. He said something about wanting to cushion my fall. I told him not to.
WILLIE. Carried that big old bump on his head for years.
PINKIE. Just laughing your head off.
WILLY. That was just like little Sam.
JES. Saigon.
PINKIE. He volunteered.
JES *(to audience)*. I was a conscientious objector.
PINKIE. How was Canada?
JES. 1968. Hot, white beach. The Bahamas.
WILLY. One of my legs is longer than the other.
PINKIE. He was a real hero. Worth his salt. Stupid as mud, but a hero just the same. Blowing up like that. He should have died over in Vietnam for his country. What'd he die for? Should have been blown to bits on some land mine, fighting someone else's battle. Instead of blowing up for... What did he die for? *(Silence.)* Don't look at me like that.

You're the one with all this stuff. *(Indicates box marked "SAM.")* Look at this. What's in here?

WILLY. Don't start stirring things up, Pinkie. Everything's packed down and ordered...

PINKIE *(in Sam's box)*. His uniform. His football trophy, basketball trophy, baseball...track...honor roll pin, medals of honor, dog tags...his varsity jacket...*(Cradling the rag.)* He blew up and wasn't enough to piece together for a decent funeral.

WILLY. Hush, Pinkie.

PINKIE. And everybody knew and nobody said a word. He said he was going to die.

WILLY. This isn't the time, Pinkie.

PINKIE. When? When, then? What did our brother die for?

WILLY. Too late now to look back. Time now to look to the future.

PINKIE. Keep your eye on the prize...And what a sweet crackerjack prize you got. Big old house, two car garage, a fence for them junkies outside to lean up on...and now you're moving to a bigger, brighter, whiter neighborhood. Leave all us po' dunk Negroes behind. You and Marva. Especially Marva, living fat.

WILLY. Everyone got theirs. You grabbed your share with both hands...

PINKIE. My children were hungry—

WILLY. Weren't we all. Enough said.

PINKIE. Let me hush.

JES. All of that is past and done. Let it go. Spit it out like a old woman's dried up tiddy. No use sucking on that. Set your teeth on the future's firm, sweet breast.

(We hear a clear, sweet bell. A light comes up on LOTTIE in her room.)

JES. Look at this—Aunt Celine's iron, Great-grandma Semple's quilt...

PINKIE. My first baby carriage...

JES. Uncle Matt's lucky horseshoe...Marva's straightening comb...Shaka Zulu's spear, I expect. And these...*(Holding up shackles.)* You're taking these?

WILLY. I'll sort things out once we get there.

(LOTTIE enters in a white dress.)

LOTTIE. We are gathered here today, though everyone isn't here yet...

PINKIE. I hope that Marva heifer doesn't show.

LOTTIE. ...to celebrate the death of...

PINKIE. BIRTH.

LOTTIE. ...to celebrate the birth of the King. "His life was the manna that fed the soul-weary masses." I read that in a book.

JES *(overlapping)*. K-A-N-I-B...I may not be able to spell it—but I know what it means.

LOTTIE. I don't remember the King. I wasn't born back then, but from the films in schools I saw the marches and the people in dashikis and 'fros, carrying signs and singing those old Negro spirituals. Those were the days of King, of Camelot, when legendary heroes arose. Women like Angela...Angela...something...Angela and her brothers in prison...Soledad. Angela Soledad.

PINKIE. Angela DAVIS.

LOTTIE. Angela Davis? Angela Davis and her sister, Patricia Lumumba.

PINKIE *(remembering, longingly)*. PATRICE Lumumba was a man.

LOTTIE. It reminds me of when we studied that French woman who fought alongside her brothers and she heard voices and bells and was burned at the stake for her beliefs.

JES. A steak sounds good. I'm hungry.

LIZA *(offstage)*. Any minute now we'll be sitting at the table. The day of feasting has arrived.

LOTTIE. And the king and his knights sat around the table...

PINKIE. What knights?

JES. Ku, klux, and klan.

LOTTIE. Jackson, Bond, and Young Andrew the lionhearted...

PINKIE. And Toto and Dorothy flew over the cuckoo's nest...Willy, I told you to let this girl grow up.

LOTTIE. In the days of Camelot there came forth a king whose holy quest took him to the mountaintop. And he looked over to the other side and heard the voices and saw the visions which he brought back to his people. He brought to them a dream. But before he could lead them to the promised land, he died. But "his life was the manna that fed the soul-weary masses." *(Blackout.)*

SCENE THREE

(We hear voices in the blackout.)

VOICES *(overlapping and repeating)*. YANG YANG YANG YANG. YANG YANG YANG. It is a far, far better thing I do than I have ever done before. All for one and one for all...Ungawa! Kings are not born: they are made of universal hallucination. Fight the power. Free Mandela. Viva Zapata. Remember the Soledad Seven. I have a dream.

(Voices are drowned out by bells. Spotlight up on JES.)

JES. I'm not bitter. I'm not hostile, I'm not angry. I'm not going to sneak into your house at night and slit your throat. I'm Jes Semple—I like white people. There are two kinds of white people. The kind-hearted liberals who subscribe to the *Village Voice, Jet Magazine,* and *Town and Country.* And then there are those that still believe Gerry Cooney is the Great White Hope. Not that the white folk can't fight. But you put a black man, who's either consciously or unconsciously aware of his over one hundred years of oppression, in the ring with a white man and he's going to beat the shit out of the white man. And he's getting paid for it, too. Just as if you put a Latino male in the ring, he's going to beat the shit out of that white man and depending on what oppressed dictatorial regime he might have come from—he'll give that black man a good whupping too. You take an American Indian—and this is the fight I personally want to see—he'll beat the shit out of all of them...with his hands tied behind his back...blindfolded. I'm not bitter, I'm not hostile. I'm not angry. Call me Jes Semple.

(LOTTIE enters the spotlight, laughing.)

LOTTIE. You're so funny, Uncle Jes.
JES. Come here, my sweet naive. Let Uncle Jes whisper in your ear. *(LOTTIE goes over to JES and he begins whispering in her ear. She laughs and laughs and laughs.)* Oh, stop, Uncle...oh, don't, stop...oh...oh...*(LOTTIE laughs until she cries...then laughs some more. Blackout.)*

SCENE FOUR

(Lights up on living room. MAMA PEARL has entered and takes C stage. LOTTIE is at the window watching PAPA TOMMY. Everyone else is in their usual positions.)

PEARL. I started out as a singer. Most of my first engagements were in the cotton fields. I was a healthy alto. I could sing. I can't anymore. *(Tries singing.)* Brighten the corner where you are... You could hear me a mile away. They used to call me Big Mouth.

LOTTIE. He's wearing a bow tie! He just got into the gate.

PEARL. Then I started sneaking to Bubba's at night—singing the blues, yeah. I was my mama's only child and this man says to me—"Girl, you sound good. Let me take you to Louisiana with me." I was sixteen at the time or I was fifteen...His name was Floyd. A piana player. He said, "Girl, you can be a great singer. Come on with me." And I said that I would first have to ask my mama.

LOTTIE. He's up to the garden.

PEARL. Next morning I told Mama that I could become a great singer if she would just let me go with Floyd to Louisiana. Don't you know that woman played those evil blues upside my head, that I will never forget. First, for sneaking out at night. Second, for wanting to sing that nasty, evil, low-down blues. Thirdly, for hanging around shiftless, lazy musicians—My daddy was a musician and had run out on Mama and me for some no account, hulley-gulley gal. And lastly, for wanting to leave her alone—me, being her only child. She beat me for seven days and seven nights.

LOTTIE. He's past the zinnias.

PEARL. After she finished beating me, she was so tired, she went to sleep. While she slept, I packed my things and took the next bus to Louisiana. I caught up with Floyd and we teamed up. We called ourselves—Big Mouth and Ivory. We toured Mississippi, Virginia, Florida and all the way up to Chicago. That's where I met your daddy. A tap-dancing fool. Talk about some quick pepper feet! As big-footed as that man is, it's amazing how fast he could move them. I met him in this club and I said, "Hey, fool, where you learn to dance like that?" He said that he knew how to tap before he learned to walk. Shoot, people remember Bojangles, the Nicholas Brothers, Sammy Davis...Sandman... your daddy was the best.

LOTTIE. He stopped.

PEARL. I quit Floyd and teamed up with your daddy. Big Mouth Pearl and Mr. Pepper Feet. We went to New York in '41 or '42.

JES/PINKIE/WILLY. '41.

LOTTIE. He's taking off his hat and pulling out a handkerchief.

PEARL. '41. We were in love. He said that he loved me more than anything in the world and that was good enough for me. So we got married and the same night we debuted at the Apollo.

LOTTIE. He's wiping his head and looking around.

PEARL. Mama wrote to tell me that she was coming up to see the fool I had married.

LOTTIE. He's at the foot of the steps.

WILLY. Maybe I should help him up.

PEARL. Let him be. He said he didn't need any help, the fool. *(Continuing.)* I met her at the train station and she beat me over the head with her suitcase. "When I woke up that morning you were gone." She moved in with us and prayed for our souls every night we went on stage.

LOTTIE. He's on the second step.

PEARL. I got pregnant with Marva, swell up so bad, I was laid up in bed. Tommy was tapping at the Cotton Club and packing them in. Mr. Pepper Feet.
LOTTIE. He's still on the second step.
PEARL. He felt it would help the act if he had a partner. I was laid up in bed. So he hired this stringy-haired, skinny gal by the name of Lola.
UNISON. Lola.

(There is a knocking on the door. LOTTIE opens the door and an ancient, shuffling, TOMMY enters.)

WILLY. Come on in. How are you, Pop?
TOMMY. Umm-hmmm. Umm-hmm.
JES. Let me rub your head for luck, old man.
TOMMY. Rub my butt.
PINKIE *(offering a seat)*. Sit over here.
TOMMY. Naw. *(He continues his slow shuffle, flapping walk past PINKIE and sits on the box labeled SAM.)*
PEARL. She thought that she was cute—that skinny, hulley-gulley child. *(TOMMY wheezes and laughs.)* Yeah, you know who I'm talking about. Lola. And she sure was LOW, wasn't she? Mr. Pepper Feet.
TOMMY *(enjoying himself)*. Dem was de days.
PEARL. Yes they were. Living in a two-room, heatless apartment with a evil mother, laid up in bed swollen to the size of a cow, and you tap-dancing at the Cotton Club with LOW-LA.
TOMMY. Yowsah, yowsah, yowsah.
PEARL. I was singing them Saint Louis Blues...Blue as I can be...
TOMMY. Dat de way. Yo' moms was a sanging fool. Bi' Mouf...

PEARL. Big Mouth and Mr. Pepper Feet.
TOMMY. De Apollo—19 and 40 somethin'.
PEARL. I told them already.
TOMMY. '41. And de Cot-tone Club.
PEARL. And LOW-LA.
TOMMY. Yowsah, yowsah, dem was de days. *(Then:)* I gots to pee.
PEARL. Who's stopping you?
TOMMY. Woman, I's tie-ud.
PEARL. And I's a bony-backed mule.
WILLY. I'll take him, Ma.
PEARL. When did he become *your* husband? *(She stands, wide-legged in front of TOMMY and squats so that he can climb on her back.)*
PINKIE. Mama, you're going to break your back.
PEARL. It'd take more than this fool to break my back.
TOMMY *(as they exit UR).* Can't you go no fast-uh?
PEARL. Man, don't you pee on me.
WILLY. Mama, I'll take him.
PEARL. I can take him.
WILLY. I'll take him.
TOMMY. Bony-back woman. Let he take me. You too slow.
PEARL. Gone, take him. The fool. *(WILLY and TOMMY exit.)* Calling somebody a bony-backed woman. That's the second time. We couldn't find a parking spot in front of the house. Too many people out front running back and forth. I parked a block away. Started walking with him on my back. His feet ain't any good anymore. He know. He called me a bony-backed woman. Said I was too slow. You talk about somebody bony...Lola was bony. She was the skinniest thing I'd ever seen. The only thing big on her was her knees. She was so skinny you could thread her through the eye of a needle except for them knees. She was

as skinny as a toothpick. Looked like somebody had used her to clean the gunk from between their teeth. She wasn't that clean. Always smelled of that toilet of Paris. She smelled like she poured that stuff all over herself to hide the fact that she didn't bathe regular. It must have gotten pretty funky up there on stage with her. Especially doing them highkicks. They must have smelled her all the way in the back row balcony. She was a skinny, musty-smelling, hulley-gulley gal. That was a long time ago. I don't know why I'm thinking about her now for. Haven't thought of her in a long time.

(WILLY re-enters.)

PINKIE. Didn't Marva buy Dad a motorized wheelchair, Mama?
PEARL. You know your father. He doesn't go for them new-fangled, electricized contraptions. He didn't want to sit in it. He didn't want to sit comfortable in somebody else's electric chair and then get fried and served up with mashed potatoes and corn bread. He said, "What did God make strong-backed womens for?" I have lost a few extra pounds but my back is still strong. We all have our crosses to bear. And as long as I'm able...
PINKIE. All I'm saying is that you shouldn't have to carry a grown man on your back.
PEARL. I didn't have to bear five big-headed children and raise them up. But I did. I didn't have to buy you new clothes and shoes while I wore the same Sears and Roebuck dress that I patched for twelve years and stuff my shoes with newspaper. But I did. I didn't have to take an extra job scrubbing floors at the Sheridan Hotel at night scraping knees on the tiles so you could get your teeth

fixed and get you that saxophone you begged me for and then played it once, deciding that you'd rather take up bongos.

UNISON. BUT I DID.

PEARL. But I did. Who stayed up all night wiping your snotty nose and giving you mustard compresses to ease the fever when you had the flu? Changed your diaper and gave you my tiddy when you were a bawling baby girl? Not that I'm complaining. You do what you are able, to provide the best for your family. Your daddy ain't heavy. Compared to the burdens I've had to shoulder in my lifetime—He's light. When are you getting married?

PINKIE. Who said anything about getting married?

PEARL. That baby sitting in your belly. I swear, Pinkie, you should give at least one of your children a name.

PINKIE. All mine have names.

PEARL. Your daddy told me that he loved me more than anything in the world and that was good enough for me. None of my children had to wonder where they came from.

PINKIE. Nobody has to wonder about mine. The truth is...

WILLY. Hush now, Pinkie.

PINKIE. Let me hush. I came here to have a nice time. Let me close my mouth. My child will speak for me one day. I'm quiet, now.

PEARL. I've been with one man for fifty years. Promised to love only me to the day he died. None of mine had to wonder.

PINKIE. Let me hush. *(We hear voices outside: "hungry"—"I'm hungry," "Spare some change..." "I want a VCR, a Porsche, and chicken in every pot..." "I feel hungry..." "My children need food." Then a rapid knocking at the door.)*

MARVA *(offstage)*. Let me in...please, open the door.

(WILLY grabs a baseball bat and opens the door. MARVA rushes in. She looks like a white woman with heavy make-up and disheveled but expensive clothes. WILLY runs out with bat.)

PEARL. What happened?
MARVA. They tried to kill me...they were going to kill me. Three black boys. They surrounded me at my car. Pulling at my purse...my hair...my suit. Calling me names. They don't know me. They don't know who I am. Calling me out of my name. Who the hell are they? Who do they think they are? No count, worthless...my hair...my suit...my car.

(WILLY re-enters.)

WILLY. Scattered like rats. That's why we're moving. This isn't what was promised.
MARVA. They tried to kill me. They shot at me.
LOTTIE. Fire-crackers.
PINKIE. No one bothered me when I came up.
MARVA. Well, I guess they wouldn't bother you.
PINKIE. And what do you mean by that?
PEARL. Marva didn't mean anything by that. You've always been so high-strung, Pinkie.
MARVA. I didn't mean anything by that, surely.
PINKIE. Surely, let me close my mouth.
PEARL. Let me look at you. What'd they do to my baby, my bright morning star...oh...*(Surveying and smoothing out the damage.)*
MARVA. It was terrible, Mama. And I wanted to look especially nice for this occasion..my nails...
PEARL. Mama kiss it. All well again—see. *(PEARL kisses MARVA's hands and face. MARVA laughs. They hug.)*

MARVA. Jonathan couldn't make it today—he was on call. He sends his regards.

JES. How is Doctor Hatchet?

PEARL. Now, Jes...Never mind him. One child crazier than the other. But he's crazy for sure. Always has been, always will be. But the Lord never gives you more than you can handle and sometimes he sweetens the pot. *(To MARVA.)* —My chocolate drop, on the cover of *Essence Magazine* this month, and once again voted Black Woman of the Year. I save the articles, put them in the scrapbook...

WILLY. I was voted Manager of the Month...gave me a plaque with my name on it.

PEARL. And your eyes—hazel?

MARVA. Blue.

PEARL. You looked so beautiful on the cover of *Jet Magazine*.

MARVA. That was the first cover I did.

PEARL. That was back when you looked like Dianne Carroll. Then for *Ebony* you looked more like Diana Ross.

MARVA. Before Diana Ross looked like Diana Ross.

PEARL. By the time she did *Vogue* she looked like a young Lena Horne.

MARVA. That was around the sixth operation. And I had just started the chemical peels. They burn away the darker outer layers...the nerve endings become so sensitive that you can't touch or be touched. They wrap you in a cocoon until you heal.

PINKIE. When you were little, they used to call you tar-baby. Big-lipped, flat-nosed, tar-baby, remember?

MARVA. I remember.

PEARL. My daughter was named "The Black Woman of the Year," three years in a row.

MARVA. I take pride in setting a standard.

PEARL. And married herself a doctor.

PINKIE. Who burned, tucked, cut and sucked all the black out of you years ago.
UNISON. HUSH, PINKIE.
PINKIE. Let me hush.
TOMMY *(offstage)*. Gits me off dis shit house.
WILLY. I'll get him. *(Exits.)*
MARVA. And how is Father?
PEARL. You know your father...
TOMMY *(offstage)*. OOOHHH, Lordy...de pain, de pain, de pain o' him-roids.
MARVA. Have you thought of a home?
PEARL. He's got a home.
LOTTIE *(who's been looking out the window)*. Sometimes I sneak out and give them things. The homeless. I give them handouts. Leftovers...bread, rice, beans...fruit to their children. Dried fruit keeps longer. Raisins.
JES. Next thing you know...they'll want a seat at the table.
LOTTIE. It makes me sad to see them. We can spare a little.

(WILLY enters carrying TOMMY.)

WILLY. We don't have enough to feed the whole damn neighborhood...
MARVA *(adjusting her face)*. Of course we do contribute to various charities...SAVE THE POOR...UNICEF...
WILLY. The whole crippled, mangy-assed breed. They're no kin to me.
MARVA. ...The Negro College Fund...NAACP...
WILLY. They're no kin to me.
MARVA. I'm a life member of the NAACP.
LOTTIE. Some live in subway tunnels...the children...I give them raisins...they give me smiles...

WILLY. I pay taxes so welfare mothers can sit at home watching the VCR.

MARVA. Just last year we adopted a boy from Ethiopia and a girl from Somalia. They're in the finest boarding school in Europe. The question is "What is to be done?" and "When have we done enough?"

TOMMY *(looking at MARVA)*. Who is you?

MARVA. Who am I? I'm your daughter, Father.

TOMMY. Youse ain't mine.

MARVA. I'm not yours? I'm your daughter, Marva, Father.

PEARL. Your eldest girl.

TOMMY. Eldest? Cain't be mine. Naw, uh-uh, cain't be mine.

LIZA *(offstage)*. All that's left is the garnish and then I'm done. Set the table everyone...the day of feasting has arrived.

UNISON. HALLELUJAH! *(All begin to set the table, finding tablecloth, dishes, and silverware among the rubble.)*

LOTTIE. We are gathered here today to celebrate the birthday of Reverend Martin Luther King.

MARVA. I was there. 1963. The march on Washington.

WILLY. I had work to do that day.

MARVA. Thousands of us walking hand in hand to the great lawn. Reverend Martin Luther King uttered his famous speech. He was a beautiful orator. Black as coals. In the heat of the revolution. America had lost its innocence—our sons were in a foreign land fighting strange battles for causes we couldn't understand. This was before the assassinations. Before LBJ threw up his hands and wept. Before the fall of Nixon, the peanut farmer, the movie star, and the lessons of Bush tactics. Back when America lost its first blush, King spoke of a vision, a dream. In the midst of bombings and fires he spoke of his vision of the future. They killed the man but his memory burns on in an eternal flame. His dream burns on in the minds of the survivors. In those frightful days, America lost its innocence in the jaws of the revolution. (And with that thought some might argue that it was our innocence that fed the revolution.) Point taken. And with the devouring of that innocence came hope. Reverend Martin Luther King Jr. had a dream. And he passed that dream on in a voice that rang out to all on that fateful day. And on that day we were all brothers and sisters...in that moment in time we were all family and holding hands. White man, Black man, Gentile, Jew, Arab, Indian...I remember sitting on that great lawn and listening to a man, a king as he cast bread upon the waters. And we sang "We Shall Overcome"...

UNISON.
> WE SHALL OVERCOME
> WE SHALL OVERCOME SOME DAY
> DEEP IN MY HEART
> I DO BELIEVE
> WE SHALL OVERCOME SOMEDAY.

(Humming as...)

PINKIE. Yes. I remember that day. I was there. I can still hear his voice. Our dream was one. It was as if he was speaking only to me, looking only at me. He knew he was going to die. The death threats were common knowledge. Who could carry on his dream? Rev. Abernathy had told me to come to the motel *(Humming stops.)* that night and I could meet him, speak with him...It had always been my dream to conceive a child that would lead his people...

UNISON. Lies...that's enough...hush!

PINKIE. And that night with the revolution burning in my thighs...*(H/)...you know it's the truth...(H/)...I laid

---

* *(H/) indicates UNISON. HUSH.*

down...(H/)...the truth will set you free...(H/)...when I laid down...

UNISON *(overlapping)*. HUSH! HUSH! HUSH! *(They sing "We Shall Overcome" with fervor as WILLY, MARVA and PEARL tie PINKIE up and tape her mouth. WILLY places her in a box. Song stops at... I DO BELIEVE.)*

PEARL. She always was high-strung.

MARVA. Fantasies...

PEARL. I always told her to settle down. No telling who all those children of hers are by. *(WILLY tapes up the box and labels it.)* No telling.

TOMMY. I's just regusted.

PEARL. I cried when Kennedy died. I don't pay any attention to all that sluttish gossip. I don't care what anybody says... I cried when King died. *(At TOMMY.)* Lord, seems like he takes the good ones early.

TOMMY. Where's Sambo?

MARVA. Who?

TOMMY. Li'l black Sambo. Now he could dance. Only one of my chirren who could feel it. Feel where he come from.

PEARL. You know he's dead, Tommy. Been dead for a while now.

MARVA. Sam.

TOMMY. That's right. Mmm-hmmm—he was good. Mmm-hmm. Lip-smacking good served up with them pancakes.

MARVA. What?

TOMMY. Pancakes. With pancakes. That's how we ate 'im.

LOTTIE *(laughing)*. Pancakes and Aunt Jemima's syrup.

WILLY. Shut up.

LOTTIE. But, Dad, it's just a joke—get it?

WILLY. Go to your room.

LOTTIE. You can't send me to my room for the rest of my life—

WILLY. Shut up. Shut him up.

MARVA. He's just an old man, talking out of his head. Sam had a proper funeral. Just close your ears, child.

JES. Though there wasn't enough of him to piece together for a decent funeral.

PEARL. He was the one that wanted to be cremated.

LOTTIE. SAMBO! PANCAKES—FRIED...

WILLY. SHUT UP! This is not the time to get into this. This is not the time.

PEARL. It was an accident. He's the one that bought the insurance.

JES. Blow your hands. Don't come crying to me.

MARVA. It was declared by the authorities as an accidental death.

JES. Don't come crying to me.

WILLY. Not murder. Not suicide.

JES. We each got a piece.

TOMMY. Legs, thighs, wings...

PEARL. He was a saint.

LOTTIE. You're joking, right? Aren't you?

JES. Some got more than others.

MARVA. We all got the same inheritance. Some used it more wisely than others. He's the one that bought—

JES. Life insurance.

MARVA *(continuing)*. No one pushed him.

WILLY *(to JES)*. For the lives of our children.

TOMMY. Paid in blood. Still gnawing on his bones.

MARVA. He was cremated.

JES. What was left of him.

TOMMY. Burnt offerings.

LOTTIE *(covering her ears and singing loudly)*. Yang yang yang yang yang yang yang yang...*(Beat.)*

MARVA *(pulls up her face)*. How do you put up with it, Mother?

PEARL. Put up with what?

MARVA *(at TOMMY)*. Him.

PEARL. That's your pa, Marva.

WILLY. He's our father.

MARVA. I was the one that was called to pay the bills when he needed the new kidney, the bladder operation...the hip joint...the gallstone operation...the bypass...the new teeth. You're trying to tell me that what's left of him is my father...this babbling, illiterate, incoherent, shuffling, head-scratching, dinosaur used to be my father but ceased to exist with Amos and Andy reruns. Yet he attaches himself to our hems as we drag him into the next century and we're supposed to continue to pay tribute by calling him our father. *(Breaking.)* You can't be my...oh...Daddy... *(Sits on his lap.)* Dad.

TOMMY *(low)*. Bastid. *(Pushes her out of his lap.)* And y'all—BASTIDS. Cain't be mine. *(Getting up.)* No ridim. No ridim. Cain't be mine. Uh-uh.

PEARL. Calm yourself.

TOMMY. Damn bastids. Git outta my way. Yeah, I feel it. Feelin' it. *(Begins to tap.)* Dat de way. Uh-uh. Dat de way. Dem was de days. *(His whole body comes to life.)* Yowsah. Dem was de days. All uh God's niggah chirren had ridim. Yeah. Dat de way, yowsah. Day knew where it come from. Day could feel it. Don't feel nothin' now. But I ain't dead...I ain't dead...naw suh...*(He taps faster and faster then drops.)*

PEARL. Tommy...Tommy.

TOMMY *(whispering)*. Dem...was...de...days. Pepper Feet... and *(Clutches his heart.)* Lo-la.

PEARL. Lola? Lola? *(Shaking his lifeless body.)* I'll kill him...I'll kill him.

MARVA *(trying to keep her face from falling apart).* He's dead. He's dead...*(WILLY gently places TOMMY in a box, tapes the box and labels it. LOTTIE covers her eyes.)*

JES *(to LOTTIE).* What happens to a dream deferred?
>Does it dry up like a raisin in the sun?
>Does it fester like a sore and then run
>Does it stink like rotten meat
>Or sugar over like a syrup sweet
>Does it sag like a heavy load—

(LOTTIE uncovers her eyes.)
>Or does it explode?

(We see smoke coming from the kitchen.)

LIZA *(offstage, hysterically repeating).* Everything is fine. I don't need any help. Soup's on. *(Smoke billows from the kitchen as everyone runs in.)*

EVERYONE. Water, more water...*(LOTTIE, hearing Joan of Arc bells, runs out the front door with armful of food to the clamoring masses.)*

LOTTIE *(as she exits, singing).* YANG YANG YANG YANG...

WILLY. More water...more water. Save the turkey. *(JES echoes.)*

PEARL. ...the ham...*(JES echoes.)*

MARVA. ...Save the chitlings...*(JES echoes.)*

PINKIE *(from inside box).* What's going on out there? Somebody let me out. I came to celebrate.

JES. Save the house, but not the mouse. Save the kitchen, keep that water pitchin'. Save Lottie, she gonna be somebody. Save the dolphins. No one can save us, from us, for us, but us...save yourself.

MARVA. I don't know what else I can do here.

PINKIE *(from inside box).* OH! I feel him...OH...
MARVA. Lottie! Lottie! *(MARVA exits after LOTTIE.)*

(We hear gunshots from outside. PEARL enters from kitchen and lays herself across TOMMY's box. A huge bone is thrown through the window, shattering the glass.)

BONETHROWER. UNGAWA! BLACK POWER!
PINKIE *(from inside box).* He's coming...Jesus...Jesus...Jesus...HE'S COMING! *(Blackout.)*

SCENE FIVE

(Spotlight up on JES. He's eating a whole pie.)

JES. You can only slice an apple pie so many ways. Somebody is always going to go home hungry.

SCENE SIX

(The room is cleared except for a few boxes—including those labeled LINEN, STEREO, PINKIE, MA, PA, and MARVA. LIZA sits in the living room wrapped in gauze from head to toe. LOTTIE sits, her white dress ragged, soiled and bloodstained.)

WILLY. Signed the papers. Ha ha. Highland Hills. This is the open door we've been waiting for. That step into the future. My little blue bird's future. We're moving. *(WILLY*

picks up a box and exits outside. LOTTIE gets up on the table and begins to do a lewd grind-dance.)
LOTTIE *(singing, bitterly).* YANG YANG YANG YANG. YANG YANG YANG.

(WILLY re-enters.)

LIZA *(from inside bandages).* Don't forget my good china.
WILLY. Yes, Liza. *(WILLY picks up a small box next to PINKIE's box. As he exits he stops, measures its weight and then curiously shakes it. Sound of a baby crying comes from within.)*

(Spotlight up on JES—he puts on a record—and watches LOTTIE's dance. We hear a recording of Martin Luther King.)

MLK. Today I want to tell the city of Selma, today I want to say to the state of Alabama, today I want to say to the people of America and the nations of the world: We are not about to turn around. We are on the move now. Yes, we are on the move and no wave of racism can stop us. The burning of our churches will not deter us. The bombing of our homes will not dissuade us. The beating and killing of our clergymen and young people will not divert us. The arrest and the release of known murderers will not discourage us. We are on the move now. Like an idea whose time has come, not even the marching of mighty armies can halt us. We are moving to the land of freedom. *(LOTTIE silently continues grind-dance.)* However difficult the moment, however frustrating the hour, it will not be long because the truth crushed to the earth will rise again. *(LOTTIE's dance becomes a stomp shuffle stomp. She picks up spear and continues with her warrior dance which evolves into a summation out of space and time evoking spirits past and present from child to woman.)*

LOTTIE. HOW LONG?

MLK. Not long, because the arc of the moral universe is long but it bends towards justice.

LOTTIE. HOW LONG?

MLK. Not long, because mine eyes have seen the glory of the coming of the Lord.

LOTTIE. HOW LONG? *(Blackout.)*

END OF PLAY

INSIDE THE BELLY
OF THE BEAST

INSIDE THE BELLY OF THE BEAST
was originally produced by The Goodman Theatre,
Chicago, Illinois on April 18, 1994.

* * * * * * * * * * * * *

My thanks to Shirley Jo Finney,
the Chicago cast,
and Beverly Robinson

INSIDE THE BELLY OF THE BEAST

A Play in One Act
For Three Men and Five Women
(playing the following roles)

CHARACTERS

WALTER GAINES
SHOESHINE MAN
DOCTOR
ELLIS
LANGLEY
SHELDON
WIFE
CHILD
MARILYN
JAMES BOND
MALICE
POLICEMEN (3)
JOHN, THE CONQUEROR (non-speaking)

Except for Walter, Shoeshine Man, Wife and Child and Malice—the actors play in white face—or white masks.

Author's Note

The style of *BELLY* is machinal / adding machine / metropolis / eraserhead-esque. There is a sense of heightened reality. It is a dark *comedy* which gets progressively darker.

The ensemble take multiple roles. They create the settings—Street...Subway...Office...with percussive soundings—calling out, whistling, tapping, clapping. The transitions are constant overlapping movement sweeping—pushing Walter from one scene into the next.

The Shoeshine Man is a constant on stage. He is a witness to Walter's journey. In the Chicago production, Shoeshine Man also played Ellis and Child. Multiple roles may vary—but I prefer that Sheldon/Bond and Malice are played by the same actor.

INSIDE THE BELLY OF THE BEAST

PROLOGUE

Red-robed ancestral SPIRITS watch WALTER read a newspaper. An ancestral SPIRIT disrobes becoming SHOESHINE MAN as JOHN THE CONQUEROR lifts his sword above his head and swings.

ENSEMBLE. Swoop...swoop...swoop...*(ENSEMBLE vanishes.)*

SCENE ONE: Shining

(WALTER, getting his shoes shined by old SHOESHINE MAN. SHOESHINE MAN sings "Follow the Drinking Gourd." WALTER, behind his newspaper, reads aloud and laughs as if reading the comics. SHOESHINE MAN snaps his rag and mumbles to himself—accenting WALTER's lines with... "Yessah!"... "mumble, grumble"... "Is dat right, hmmph."... "mumble, grumble"...)

WALTER. ...Three slain in drive-by shooting...black Mercedes filled with black teens with gold chains and gold teeth...drove by Jamaican neighborhood at three o'clock Sunday morning...*(Laughs.)*...the two burglars broke into the elderly couple's home...described as the black Mutt and Jeff duo...got away with the elderly couple's jewelry, silverware and gold fillings...*(Laughs.)*...serial rapist...six foot five...wild bulging eyes...nappy, matted hair...discolored teeth...black...black skin...*(Laughing.)*...found that the coke-snorting African-American mayor...*(SHOESHINE MAN spits on WALTER's shoe—disgusted—and continues polishing.)*...the fallen American hero...cut off their heads...the Africanized killer bees first spotted in South America have, over the past ten years, moved upward...attacked a small quiet American suburb killing several dogs...distraught owners..."poor Spotty"...and the children...

SHOESHINE MAN. Done. Shoe is done.

WALTER *(folding newspaper. Puts it in briefcase)*. Thank you.

SHOESHINE MAN. Most folks, you can read where they came from by they shoes. Where they came from. What they had for breakfast. If they got secrets hiding behind a door. Your shoes...

WALTER. New. New shoes.

SHOESHINE MAN. Brand spanking new. *(WALTER smiles. Pays him.)*

SCENE TWO: Walter On the Street

WALTER. Taxi! Taxi! Taxi! Taxi...

SCENE THREE: Self Exam

(The DOCTOR (female) has both arms in a sling.)

DOCTOR. Mr. Walter Gaines. Please come in. This is a required routine exam for new officers of the company. Just relax.

WALTER. But how do you...

DOCTOR. You will do it. Do you mind...

WALTER. No, I...

DOCTOR. Do you mind if I smoke?

WALTER. Well, it's...

DOCTOR. It's been a hell of a day and it's just started. Do you mind?

WALTER. No.

DOCTOR. Take my cigarette out of my top pocket. *(He does so. Placing the cigarette in her mouth.)* Thank you. Now take off my right shoe. *(He does so.)* Thank you. The matches are on the counter. *(He lights the cigarette.)* Now, take off your clothes and put on the gown. *(He does so as the DOCTOR smokes taking long drags, holding the cigarette with her right foot.)*

WALTER. But there's no...I thought smoking was bad for your health, Doctor.

DOCTOR. Good. You have a sense of humor. You can write that down on your report. Go on. *(WALTER writes this on his report.)* Are you on any medication? Write down your response. Take the flashlight and the popsicle stick in your mouth...there's a mirror behind you...and say "ahh."

WALTER. ...Ahh.

DOCTOR. Tongue...tonsils...throat...OK? *(WALTER nods "yes.")* Open your eyes wide and turn on the flashlight... What do you see?

WALTER. Nothing.

DOCTOR. Good. Good. Take the stethoscope...What do you hear?

WALTER. Pounding.

DOCTOR. Ah. A heart. Please make notes. The tape measurer—for the final circumference of your head. *(Then:)* There are more female doctors today than there were ten years ago—Only ten years ago—Did you notice that, Walter?

WALTER. Yes. I noticed.

DOCTOR. Also measure your neck, waist, thighs—the length of your feet. *(Then:)* Women used to be nurses—that was good enough for them. Not anymore—Correct?

WALTER. I guess.

DOCTOR. Things change. A man competes with a female. In my day a man was dominant. Now he must compete with lesser creatures. Tested against weaker species. Is this true or false? You're hesitant. Never mind me. Note down your answer! The report is confidential. *(Then:)* You were downstairs since how long, Walter?

WALTER. Since college. Mid-management the past six years.

DOCTOR. Good. Very good. The step up you've worked so hard for. Vice-president.

WALTER. Yes. Section a22. *(Then:)* Your arms...

DOCTOR. Broken. Blood pressure. Four o'clock this morning, heading for my first shift—I was hailing a cab when a pack of them attacked me. Five of them. The oldest couldn't have been more than thirteen. Hairless black faces. A pack of growling animals. Someone called the police. They apprehended all of them. Spread-eagled on the sidewalk—shackled—the cops offered to let me stomp them. My attackers looked up at me, their girlish faces yelped as I kicked each one of the them before the cops dragged them away. *(Pause.)* Does my story offend you?

WALTER. You were attacked.

DOCTOR. Yes. It doesn't make you angry—what I did to them?

WALTER. They mean nothing to me.

DOCTOR. Note down your answer. You have high recommendations. Vice-president. High visibility position. Note down your pressure. You worked hard to get where you are.

WALTER. Yes.

DOCTOR. Family history.

WALTER. Healthy stock.

DOCTOR. No hereditary ailments?

WALTER. No.

DOCTOR. Psychological impairments?

WALTER. No.

DOCTOR. Grandparents?

WALTER. Yes.

DOCTOR. Yes. Your humor has been duly noted. Are they still living?

WALTER. My grandmother died at the age of ninety-nine in her sleep. My grandfather died earlier.

DOCTOR. Earlier.

WALTER. Gangrene.

DOCTOR. Oh?

WALTER. My father...

DOCTOR. Gangrene?

WALTER. Yes.

DOCTOR. And your father...

WALTER. Hanged. *(Pause.)* My mother died of grief. Shall I write this down?

DOCTOR. It's already in your files. *(Pause.)* Hold your balls in your right hand—look over your left shoulder and cough. *(WALTER does.)* Now, bend over. *(WALTER hesitates. Then laughs. The DOCTOR laughs.)*

SCENE FOUR: Sounds of the City

(WALTER stands on street corner.)

WALTER. Taxi! Taxi! Taxi!

SCENE FIVE: The Office

(WALTER with a box of his belongings. ELLIS is there.)

ELLIS. The new boss.
WALTER. Vice-President of Section a22.
ELLIS. I'm Ellis. Jane Ellis. Nice to meetcha.
WALTER. Ellis.
ELLIS. The new boss.

(LANGLEY wheels himself on. He has no legs.)

LANGLEY. Mr. Vice-President Walter Gaines. Jeff Langley. I was in the race for that seat but you obviously beat me to it. Better luck next time, I always say. Welcome to the department.
WALTER. Langley, thank you.
ELLIS. He's the new boss.
LANGLEY. Why don't you go get a couple of cups of java, Ellis?

ELLIS. Yeah, sure. *(To WALTER.)* Want a donut?

WALTER. No thanks.

ELLIS. Coffee without a donut?

LANGLEY. He's a Jehovah's Witness. Just fry up some coffee.

ELLIS. Sure. *(Exits.)*

LANGLEY. Yeah. No hard feelings about the job, Gaines. I got no hard feelings. I want you to know that.

WALTER. Yes. Me either.

LANGLEY. WHY SHOULD YOU! You're the one in the seat. Mr. Vice-President. Nice seat. They cushioned it real good. They make sure of that. Nice and cushy. Yeah. Anyways. I'll make myself available—walk you around. You need anything—I'll fill you in. Anything. I'm in the know. No hard feelings. *(Pause.)* You and me should stick together—you know. *(Conspiratorially.)* My name used to be—Manuel. *(We hear a crash.)*

VOICE *(from offstage)*. LANGLEY!

LANGLEY. Manuel Negril.

(SHELDON enters. He is blind.)

SHELDON. LANGLEY! You shit-head.

LANGLEY. Nice to see you too. This here is the new vice-president of operations. Walter...

SHELDON. Oh, hello, Mr. Walter.

LANGLEY. Walter Gaines.

SHELDON. Sorry barging in, sir. It's just...I think you should know from the beginning what a little kidder we have in our Mr. Langley, here. He likes to rearrange the office furniture every once in a while. Quite the kidder.

LANGLEY. Oh, stop. You love it.

SHELDON. I know that you're the one that gave Seymore those laxatives.

LANGLEY. He named his dog Seymore.

SHELDON. He steals office supplies and sells them to his cousin Tony.

LANGLEY. Oh...You see so much.

SHELDON. Even without eyes I can see that you are very short. Very ugly and very short.

LANGLEY. What kind of impression do you want to give the new vice-president, Sheldon? Sheldon is a little stressed—Must be that time of the month—Huh, Shelly?

(ELLIS enters.)

ELLIS. Two cups of coffee—fried. *(She takes donut out of her pocket.)* Just in case you changed your mind. The new boss.

WALTER. This is Section a22?

ELLIS. The new boss.

SHELDON. a22.

WALTER. This is Section a22.

LANGLEY. a22.

ELLIS. You're the boss.

LANGLEY. The big honcho.

SHELDON. You have the power to hire and fire anyone at will.

LANGLEY. El Huevos Grande.

WALTER. I'm the vice-president of Section a22.

ELLIS *(sharpening pencils)*. That's us—Section a22, yep.

WALTER. Well. Let's get to it. Ellis, what do you do?

ELLIS. I'm sharpening your pencils now. I like sharpening pencils. Then I guess...I don't know...What do you want me to do?

LANGLEY. Can you sharpen mine, next? Ellis is office manager for Section a22. Shelly...here...

SHELDON. I'm filing a complaint. He should be fired-demoted-transferred-disciplined. He's impossible.

LANGLEY. Your mother.

SHELDON. It's abuse. Mr. Gaines—either he goes, or I go. *(Pause.)* I'll give you some time to think about it. *(SHELDON exits.)*

LANGLEY. Don't worry about him. We'll have kissed and made up by lunch. He's a good accountant, Sheldon. Ellis here...

ELLIS. Done. I'll do your pencils now, Langley. *(ELLIS exits.)*

LANGLEY. Swell gal. A. little slow on the uptake but tell her what you want and she will do it by the letter. Very meticulous. Me—I'm the information center. Anything you want to know—need something to be followed up on—I'm the legman.

WALTER. I graduated with honors. Was hired here right out of college. Steady honors, citations, promotions...bonuses...Last week they told me—Vice-president Section a22. Ten years. Got the wife. The kids. Two cars. Nice home in a small, quiet American suburb. With no mortgage. Mine. Platinum cards. Vice-president of Level A, Section 22.

LANGLEY. Cushy. Nice and cushy. Name used to be Manuel Negril. Used to be six foot five. One hundred eighty-six pounds. Linebacker. Fast. Number one draft choice—And then there was the war. I volunteered. POW. They did things to me—Came home—decorated with honors. Hired out of the military, man.

(ELLIS enters carrying a cake. She exits and quickly returns with presents.)

ELLIS. PRESENTS, EVERYBODY! SHELDON, PRESENTS! PRESENTS!
LANGLEY. They send us gifts all the time. They like to keep us happy here. All the time...

(SHELDON enters. ELLIS lights the cake.)

ELLIS. Make a wish.
ALL. Wish! *(They blow out candles. ELLIS hands out presents. SHELDON opens his—A gold Viewmaster. ELLIS opens hers—A gold lamé g-string. LANGLEY opens his—Gold pair of tap shoes. WALTER opens his—Golden crown. They look at the gifts—look at each other. They laugh.)*

SCENE SIX: Walter on the Street

WALTER. TAXI! TAXI! TAXI!

SCENE SEVEN: Home

(We hear babies crying. WIFE is setting dinner.)

WALTER. You're getting fat, Louise.
WIFE. Everyday fatter and fatter and fatter.
WALTER. Not again.
WIFE. Oh, yes. Again and again and again.
WALTER. But how?

WIFE *(shrugs)*. Nothing's foolproof.
WALTER. Louise.
WIFE. Yes, Walter…*(Pause. Then:)* I went to a sale today. You should have seen it, all of us clawing our way through the designer labels. Look, Walter, I broke a nail. Little Bobby has an ear infection. He toddles around and then falls over—splat—I took him to the doctor. It's the infection—he's lost his balance. The twins have colic—one on each titty—while I warm a bottle for little Charlie—Sarah constantly hangs on to my skirt, but she's allergic to cotton. Fatter and fatter gnawing inside me—Lonnie wants to go to MIT when he grows up—Lester to Harvard—Mary wants a new red bike. And Felix…
WALTER. Louise. *(Pause.)*
WIFE. Wally. You remember when I first called you Wally?
WALTER. Wally the tadpole—
WIFE. Yes—you remember—Tadpole Wally—You remember why—you don't remember. The first time you were inside me—you grew up inside me newborn—I kissed you—my frog—You were supposed to turn into…
WALTER. Things haven't turned out like we imagined Louise.
WIFE. I kissed you and…well…Did I tell you, your son Wilbur was killed in a drive-by shooting? Our Jessica's been missing for five days now…and your precious Mayline's hiding crack vials in her underwear drawer—Frank shot his algebra teacher—the principal sent a note. Tabatha needs braces…you didn't even notice she doesn't smile anymore?
WALTER *(looking at the other room)*. The babies are crying. *(Pause.)* The babies are crying. *(Pause.)* The babies are crying. *(WIFE turns to WALTER. She kisses him and exits to the other room. WALTER eats his dinner.)*

(CHILD runs in—crying.)

CHILD. GIMME GIMME GIMME GIMMEE...*(WALTER watches.)*
WALTER. Louise. Louise.
CHILD. GIMME GIMME GIMME GIMME...
WALTER. Are you hungry?
CHILD. HUNGRY HUNGRY HUNGRY HUNGRY...*(WALTER gives CHILD his plate. CHILD eats. WALTER reads his paper. CHILD finishes eating.)* GIMME GIMME GIMME AAAAAHHHH...
WALTER. I'll tell you a story. You know the story you like—

(Child stops crying. JOHN THE CONQUEROR appears with sword raised above his head.)

WALTER. Mighty John the Slayer.
CHILD. He killed 10,000.
WALTER. When he returned home there was a parade in his honor. John the Conqueror. They roasted 200 pigs and 400 cows and the best of the harvest was his. And 10,000 pieces of gold.
CHILD. He killed 10,000.
WALTER *(swinging with imaginary sword)*. SWOOP SWOOP SWOOP SWOOP—he cut off their heads.
CHILD. He killed 10,000.
WALTER. To save ten times more. A mighty warrior. Fearless and strong. The people had awaited his birth for 10,000 years.
CHILD. SWOOP SWOOP SWOOP SWOOP—
WALTER *(passionately)*. He killed 10,000.
WALTER and CHILD. SWOOP SWOOP SWOOP—*(Swoops stop when the crying stops from the other room. Then the CHILD, exhausted, curls up on the floor.)*

(WIFE enters. Her hand is bleeding.)

WIFE. The babies are cutting teeth.
ALL. SWOOP SWOOP SWOOP SWOOP.

SCENE EIGHT: The Spy

(WALTER throwing up. Finally sits on toilet with his newspaper as MARILYN enters. She has a gun. BOND enters and sits down.)

MARILYN. Are you surprised?
WALTER *(as James Bond)*. No. I knew you would catch on to me eventually.
MARILYN. 007.
BOND. Bond. James Bond.
MARILYN. We've known all along there was a spy amongst us. We've been watching you very closely for a long time—waiting for you to expose yourself.
WALTER *(BOND lip syncs)*. But I was perfect.
MARILYN. Yes. You were. You had me convinced that you loved me, Jimmy.
BOND. Perhaps I had convinced myself.
MARILYN. That would have made you a traitor. Wouldn't it? I don't know who I hate worse—a spy or a traitor. *(BOND begins to wipe off white face/or take off mask.)* Why? Tell me why.
BOND. It was my grandfather.
MARILYN. The one that died of gangrene...
BOND. It was he who caused the trouble. On his deathbed he called my father to him and said, "Son, after I'm gone I want you to keep up the good fight. I never told you but

our life is a war and I have been a traitor all my born days. A spy in the enemy's country ever since I give up the gun in reconstruction. Live with your head in the lion's mouth. I want you to overcome them with yesses, undermine them with grins, agree 'em to death and destruction. Let them swaller you till they vomit or bust wide open." Then he died. Grandfather spoke of his meekness as a dangerous activity.

WALTER *(BOND lip syncs)*. It became a constant puzzle which lay unanswered in the back of my mind.

BOND. I was praised and rewarded for my conduct. You loved me for it.

MARILYN. But desired you to act just the opposite—you should have been more sulky and mean.

WALTER. And that would have been what they wanted.

MARILYN. I swallowed you.

BOND. Even though they were fooled and thought they really wanted me to act as I did. It made me afraid that some day they would look upon me as a traitor and I would be lost.

MARILYN. Do you love me, Jimmy? Do you love me? Tell me—

BOND. I was more afraid to act any other way because they didn't like that at all. *(MARILYN points gun at BOND.)* The old man's words were like a curse. *(MARILYN and BOND kiss.)*

MARILYN. Now who's swallowed who? *(WALTER, on toilet, grunts.)*

SCENE NINE: Walter on the Street

WALTER. Taxi! Taxi! Taxi!

SCENE TEN: Underground Railroad

(WALTER with newspaper, very uncomfortable. MALICE is there.)

MALICE *(reading a magazine).* Michele, I told you before—don't be wearing that Spandex shit. You're a big star—too big a star to be showing yourself in that shit. I told you—quit that shit. Now listen to me. And call me on Wednesday. *(He flips a page.)* Hey, sweetheart. Yeah, I'm talking to you! What's your name? Ahh, Sabrina. That's a pretty, pretty name. You like movies—uh—huh. Old movies—me too. We should go see a movie sometime—you know, maybe walk in the park. You'd like that. Or take a boat ride. Yeah?—Yeah—Oh, you are just too funny. Stop. You are just too funny. *(He licks the page.)* I'm not moving too fast am I? Come home with me. Meet the parents. *(He rips out the page and stuffs it into his pants.)* Sabrina...(To WALTER.) This is a private moment, thank you. You some kind of pervert? What you think you lookin' at? *(WALTER turns away.)* Never mind him, Sabrina. Make yourself at home. There's a Coke in the fridge...no, over there on the right. *(Back to magazine.)* I am tired of you. You have the nerve to show your face again—Lie to me again—"no new taxes..." *(Punches magazine.)* Tell me another—"no government intervention..." *(Punches magazine again.)* I told you...*(Takes out nail clippers and stabs magazine.)* Lying to me—Can't lie without a tongue. I can't hear you now, joker. Joker, I can't hear you. Can't lie without a tongue, can you, can you—what—can you? *(He flips page.)* I hated that joker...Yeah, I'm doing fine, and you? Haven't seen you in a while...just hanging, you know...and you—damn, thought you was dead...*(Turns to WALTER.)* And what are you reading, man?

WALTER. The newspaper.

MALICE. What you doing?

WALTER. Excuse me?

MALICE. Down here? Couldn't catch a cab?

WALTER. Well...

MALICE. You couldn't catch a damn cab. Cab wouldn't stop for you, huh? You flash them some green? Some nigger greens with collards and they still wouldn't stop for your black ass. Down here in the bowels. Running down here in the bowels. Damn taxis. What do you think...man...what do you think...you got some threads...Nice suit. Polo fuckin' perfume. Lookit them shoes. Damn. Them's some nice shoes, man. Why you look at me like that, man? Yeah, I stink—I stink. You married?

WALTER. Yes.

MALICE. You got a white one, don't you?

WALTER. No. She's black. My children are black.

MALICE. Shoulda got you a white one. See. Meet my girlfriend...Sabrina. Pretty. She pretty, ain't she? Pretty. Pretty. She say, Malice, you my man. The man—Malice, my sweetheart, my baby, baby, baby. Don't get me wrong now. I like black women. I love my black sister but there's a difference. A world of difference. Don't want to be politically incorrect but the difference see is, you know what I mean. You know what I mean—you are successful, see, I walk down the street with a white girl and sisters be giving me mucho smack, see, like they don't know. You understand. They don't know when you are successful it's rare to see a black woman in your environs—talking the white environ. You want to make it in the white world to be accepted universally. See, so you in this white environ and

all you see is white. Predominately white women. So who are you going to date? It's a process of natural selection. You're in that arena, right—you get comfortable in that arena, that rap, that style, that texture—you get comfortable—then boom—you try to move back into the hood. You no longer comfortable. You don't know how to talk smack—walk that walk—you don't know what the joke is—where the joke is—when to laugh. You know. You feel alienated. You know what I mean.
WALTER. Yes.
MALICE. See, niggers don't know. White folks know the game. A black woman always wants you to be proving something. It's a cultural thing. Sister say, Oh you think you successful—you may be successful but don't come this way with that successful crap. Think you running something 'cause I got news for you—You have to prove to me why I should be giving you my time and energy. Tell me why you want to be with me and you better be convincing. White women—they come at you a little different. They like to rub you the right way. Hey, sweetheart—you are successful. I want to be with you 'cause you are successful. The game is how do I get you and keep you happy. That's part of their culture. White folks give you credit. They'll suck your butt, let you know you are the baddest cat around. They show you appreciation. Invite you yachting. Come on, man, go golfing with us this weekend. We appreciate you. Who you are. Be with us...Be one of us...Be us. And as long as you do that do—it's groovy. You know what I'm saying. You are in and it is groovy. You know.
WALTER. Yes.
MALICE. We understand each other.
WALTER. Yes.

MALICE. We see eye to eye. *(The train rumbles through a tunnel. In the blackness we hear a fight—scuffling, shouts. When the light comes back on MALICE is kicking WALTER who is on the ground. MALICE has WALTER's jacket and new shoes. MALICE throws his magazine at WALTER.)* My dreams...Taxi! *(The train stops and MALICE exits. The train continues.)*

WALTER. Help...help...God, help me.

(The train stops. Three POLICEMEN get on the train.)

POLICEMAN 1 *(to WALTER)*. OK, get up. *(Casually kicks WALTER.)* Get up, Malice.

WALTER. No...no, I'm Walter...Walter Gaines...I called for help...

POLICEMAN 2. Sure, sure, we're takin' you in.

POLICEMAN 3. Get up, Malice. *(He kicks him again.)*

WALTER. No...my name is Walter Gaines...Let me...*(He reaches inside... the POLICEMEN draw their weapons.)* No...Wait...I'm getting my ID.

POLICEMAN 2. No games, Mal.

WALTER. Let me get my ID. Please, Officer. *(POLICEMAN 1 nods OK. WALTER looks for his ID.)* He took it. He took my ID. He stole my ID.

POLICEMAN 3. Come along now, Mal.

WALTER *(hysterical)*. He has my ID. He knows where I live. He'll kill my wife...my children...He'll go to my job... *(Trying to escape. The POLICEMEN surround him—beating him. The train runs through a tunnel into blackness.)*

SCENE ELEVEN: Laying on of Hands

(WALTER, unconscious on the ground. JOHN THE CONQUEROR appears and remains through end of play. Red-robed ANCESTORS witness as SHOESHINE MAN performs a "laying on of hands" on WALTER.

NOTE: The last scenes: Trail of the Beast, Swallowed by the Beast and Recognition, are Ionescue/Kafka-esque. WALTER at first sees himself as warrior hunting down the beast. He comes eye-to-eye and is swallowed by the beast. He then recognizes that he is the beast and with that recognition comes his humanity. He becomes in his final moment—Ralph Ellison's Invisible Man—waiting for the right moment to emerge.

SCENE TWELVE: Trail of the Beast

(Spotlight up on WALTER.)

ALL. Swoop. Swoop. Swoop. Swoop. Swoop.
WALTER. He took his time following the fresh footprints he left in the snow. Smelling him out. O mighty conqueror, they had cried. O redeemer. Savior. Ten thousand years they had waited for his birth. Smelling him out. *(Light out on WALTER.)*

SCENE THIRTEEN: Swallowed by the Beast

(Spotlight up on WALTER.)

WALTER. Eyes. Skin. Armor. Smoking nostrils. Mouth opened wide and swallowed me whole. Inside. Inside the constricted throat. The water, waste. Inside. The bowels. Retching. An arm. Torso. A head with eyes dangling from sockets and mouth agape. *(Light out on WALTER.)*

SCENE FOURTEEN: Recognition

(Spotlight up on WALTER.)

WALTER. Inside. The skin. Scaly armor. Inside. Me. Staring out from under the heavy guarded lids. Lips. Legs. Arms. Blackened Armor. Heart pounding. An old man sings something...somewhere. A passageway. Light approaches. I blink. My head. The mouth open. Breathes in...Inside. Me. Inside. Me. Waiting. *(Blackout.)*

END OF PLAY

DIRECTOR'S NOTES

DIRECTOR'S NOTES